AF255730

CUP MY DAYS LIKE WATER

The Poiema Poetry Series

Poems are windows into worlds; windows into beauty, goodness, and truth; windows into understandings that won't twist themselves into tidy dogmatic statements; windows into experiences. We can do more than merely peer into such windows; with a little effort we can fling open the casements, and leap over the sills into the heart of these worlds. We are also led into familiar places of hurt, confusion, and disappointment, but we arrive in the poet's company. Poetry is a partnership between poet and reader, seeking together to gain something of value—to get at something important.

Ephesians 2:10 says, "We are God's workmanship . . ." *poiema* in Greek— the thing that has been made, the masterpiece, the poem. The Poiema Poetry Series presents the work of gifted poets who take Christian faith seriously, and demonstrate in whose image we have been made through their creativity and craftsmanship.

These poets are recent participants in the ancient tradition of David, Asaph, Isaiah, and John the Revelator. The thread can be followed through the centuries—through the diverse poetic visions of Dante, Bernard of Clairvaux, Donne, Herbert, Milton, Hopkins, Eliot, R. S. Thomas, and Denise Levertov—down to the poet whose work is in your hand. With the selection of this volume you are entering this enduring tradition, and as a reader contributing to it.

—D.S. Martin
Series Editor

Cup My Days like Water

ABIGAIL CARROLL

CASCADE *Books* • Eugene, Oregon

CUP MY DAYS LIKE WATER

The Poiema Poetry Series

Cascade Books
An Imprint of Wipf and Stock Publishers
199 W. 8th Ave., Suite 3
Eugene, OR 97401

www.wipfandstock.com

PAPERBACK ISBN: 978-1-6667-6289-1
HARDCOVER ISBN: 978-1-6667-6290-7
EBOOK ISBN: 978-1-6667-6291-4

Cataloguing-in-Publication data:

Names: Carroll, Abigail, author.

Title: Cup my days like water / by Abigail Carroll.

Description: Eugene, OR: Cascade Books, 2023 | The Poiema Poetry Series

Identifiers: ISBN 978-1-6667-6289-1 (paperback) | ISBN 978-1-6667-6290-7 (hardcover) | ISBN 978-1-6667-6291-4 (ebook)

Subjects: LCSH: subject | subject | subject | subject

Classification: call number 2023 (print) | call number (ebook)

03/28/23

To all who pray, and to those who have yet to find their prayer

Contents

The Word Tastes Like Sun–Crammed Plums

plucked from an orchard on the north side
of a hill, dew-laced by the chill of star-pierced
August nights; jam on seeded toast, thickly
humming with the mission of bees, hinting
what the light was like in Eden, brimming
with life's flurry. When I swallow the Word
it sings—a warbler in my chest tuning me
to new scales, fluting the song of universe,
which is also the song of who I am. At night,
the Word recites itself to my sleeping bones
in whispered owl tones, sweeps away silt,
filters slag, grit, regret. With me is the Word
before I wake, sowing hunger, holding flame.

> *You chew on Scripture day and night.*
>
> —PS 1:2

Only Ask

and I will cool your tongue
with water from clean depths of the lake
that is forever.
Only ask,
and I will set a table of peace between you
and fear,
and the candle of my presence
will burn through the night-veil
of your dimmest hour.
Only ask,
and my hushed gaze
will become a shelter
more vast than the watch of winter stars,
stronger than sun's tomorrow.
Yours is forest and sea, yours
a gratuity of days,
each one jeweled, wine-red,
glittering, rare.
Yours, the compass rose
of my voice pointing north, pointing due
rest, due light, due song.
Yes, only ask,
and I will breathe your new name
across the flush tabula

of dawn, bear you
across the wide threshold of time,
let you in on the laughter
by which nebulae are formed.

> *Only ask, and I will give you the nations as your inheritance,*
> *the whole earth as your possession.*
>
> —PS 2:8

Curtain Me in Silence

Mute my lips,
the voices tenanting
my head. Only here
is safety: losing
my say, forgetting
how to fend,
beg, argue, claim.
Make me lamb,
make me leavened bread,
make me phlox,
purple and white.
Oh teach me
to be winter night,
to wait like stars wait,
to be lost,
to be found
within the shield,
glory all around.
And I will break
into who I am,
empty of all noise,
all blast—

a bowl holding
no thing more
than what rises,
what communions,
what lasts.

Wading Through Milkweed

in rubber boots to where the land looks
across clover fields,
stove-black cows.
Peering into the loamy eye
of the neighbor's wild-maned horse.
Lying on the knobby earth.
Letting the ground
press its messages into my back,
leaves the color of claret
staircasing the wind.
Opening ear to sky,
to grass song, the *churr*
and scold of fan-tailed wrens.
Here, my prayer begins.

> *The Lord hears.*
>
> —PS 4:3

Prayer as an Assemblage of Souvenirs

The lamp
by which I enter night.
Sedum, the color of dusk,
holding its own against time.
By what am I to measure
this life?

A gallery of taped-up cards:
memoir in small art
and script.
Five stones from an island
in Maine, worn smooth
as the flowing of my days.

Empty bell vase
in which twelve monarchs
dried their wings.
A blue-glazed mug of pens—
fine-tipped tools
for the naming of hours.

> *Every morning I lay out the pieces of my life on your altar.*
>
> —PS 5:3

Darkness Snagged My Bones

Small at first,

like a spiny brown burr snags

a coat hem, a fine

wool skirt. Like mice

in winter, it moved into the dusky

wall voids of my frame,

settled deep

in the breezy shade of my lungs.

Now it travels my blood,

pebbles my voice,

a country of perpetual mist

and dim.

At night, the ache of it chants

its Cimmerian song,

lets on about its little wins.

It taunts.

> *O Lord, heal me, for my bones are troubled.*
>
> —PS 6:2

Justice is a Song on the Lips

of the hosed down,
the spat on,
the stolen from,
the falsely named.
And what is a song
but a rising up
like fire
of what is true—
a prophetic hymn?
A song is stronger
than bars, lives longer
than lies, holds
its own against
stark offices of hate.
No weapon
forged against it
can stand.
Even spilled blood
sings.

> *Open your eyes, my God;*
> *hear my plea for justice once and for all.*
>
> —PS 7:6

My Life is the Candle I Lift

What am I
but fallout
of star-furnace
and a lover's
half-sighed
word,
glint
in the dying
white tail
of a comet,
blurred?

> *What are mere human beings that you think about them?*
> —PS 8:4

Such is the Heart

The ache of combing strangers' eyes
for a lost map.
A hymn hummed low.
Years yearning
for salt air and the plaintive
ritual of tide.
A dented tin cup—never quite full.
A thorn staving off
every false word, every
too-kind hand.
A record, grooved,
looping all manner of slip-up,
rehearsing doubt.
A cherry wood harp, tuned
and levered,
waiting for the madrigal to start.

> *I will praise the Lord with my whole heart.*
>
> —PS 9:1

Where is the Lord?

Always hiding—
a well deep in the earth,
a herring gull's feather, white,
waiting to be picked up.
Where is the Lord?
Always riding
the space between
breath and branches, light-years
and stars—
the bright, slow rendering
of who we were into who
we at last are.

Where is the Lord?
Always in song
behind a curtain, behind
a wall,
behind a truth too tall to scale.
Yes, always behind a strong veil,
a fire screen,
a heat shield by which we're spared
the brunt of a vast love—
scouring, wild.

> *O Lord, why do you stand so far away?*
> —PS 10:1

Net Me in Your Gaze

Set me before your eyes, no thing
left to hide.
Unsheathe all that's shadowed, disguised.
You mind the land,
the deep.
Day after day, you probe the ocean
of my heart, flag silent caverns
untouched by light
where sightless
creatures move and work
stark designs.
Why do I run from your love?
Why do I fear being seen by one
who saw me made?

> *He observes everyone on earth.*
>
> —PS 11:4

May the Blowsy Scent of Lilacs

opening in spring
silence empires of lies. May infants
babbling against their mother's chests prophesy.
May a single drop of rain
on the cheek of the fabulist, the fraud,
cause a chance looking up.
May night canticle what is true
over the sleeping dreams
of a slander-weary land. May a radish seed
outdo the proud, the big-mouthed,
all manglers of facts. Yes,
may the smooth-tongued suddenly forget
their words, unlearn speech.
May mute fish sing.

> *May the Lord silence all flattering lips*
> *and every boastful tongue.*

> —PS 12:3

How Long

till borders vanish from the map,
highway signs flashing DUI deaths instead announce
sightings of rare birds
in both English and Latin names?
How long till earthquakes cease, phone alerts
report not a missing child,
but sticky-hand sisters with bannered stand
selling lemonade?
How long till lies become extinct,
all running water sings clean,
hospitals are converted into art museums?
How long till nothing's left for the evening news
but the naming of stars,
the tracking of wild gorilla clans,
school kids hammering boats out of bomber drones?
How long till we see
the dream sleeping in our bones?
Oh, tell me, how long till spring?

> *How long, O Lord?*
> —PS 13:1

Is There Not One

who lives lightly on the earth,
who thinks also of snails
sharing the rain-wet road,
of geese circling for a place
to land? Is there not one
who prays for the seam-sewers
of jeans sweating
in buzzing lofts,
not one who asks the Father
to dazzle them
with guava, star fruit,
yogurt, dates?
Is there not one who weeps
for grace, who stays up late
plotting art
for the rooms
of the newly born—
shells, perhaps,
wave-buffed gratuities of the sea
daubed in mauves
and Spanish blue?

> *The Lord looks down from heaven . . .*
> *to see if anyone seeks God.*
>
> —PS 14:2

What is Asked of Me

To lift the screen and let the buzzing fly
escape. Not be caught up in things too lofty
for me. Read—feed my mind with prose
in books that candle the night. Leave no morsel
in the fridge to rot. Honor the sweat of labor
unseen. When driving, sing, sing, sing, sing,
sing. Daily shape silence in which another
might speak. Dare to say *no* a hundred times
in order to say *yes* to what's right. Salve
the bruised. Be no thing but myself. Write.

> *Who may enter your presence on your holy hill?*
> *Those who lead blameless lives and do what is right.*

> —PS 15:2

Appointment With Stillness

Stand in the company
of a tree.
You will want to run fast and far.
Stay.
Remain in the arbor's under-gaze
as under the eye-watch
of love.
Don't be surprised if
you are unable to move,
stunned
by a vast silence
redolent of apples and rain
and the precise scent of air on the day
you were born.
Learn to concede
to the slanted light.
In time, you will sink to the ground,
let bark imprint its longhand
on your back.
In time,
leaves and winged insects
will cantillate
their shimmering truths.

In time,
you will know yourself to be held
by what cannot be seen—
the white pappus of a dandelion
lifted on a playful breeze.

    In your presence is fullness of joy.

    —PS 16:11

I Saw the Likeness of the Lord

Once in a shop—
almonds of glass
dangled in the window,
re-choreographing light.
All was awash in colors native
to Eden, colors cached
in geodes,
plumage, dreams.
I saw the Lord's likeness once
on an apple-scented day,
wind-breaker flapping
as I pumped the rope swing
under a tree on a mown field
at the Cape, dulcimer notes
thinly riding the air,
gliding, playing me like a fine,
shiny instrument.
Once, I saw the likeness of the Lord
on a cold northern beach:
empty, stony, wild—
seals eyeing me

as I perched on the lip of the shore,

everything mine,

the faceted roll

and swell of tide, glory

churning deep, carving in me a hold

for the sweep, the joy, the brine.

> *When I awake,*
> *I will be satisfied with seeing your likeness.*
>
> —PS 17:15

At Eight, I Thought God Lived in the Rafters

My eyes fixed on the cross-
beams converging in the church's apex,
pointing like an arrow to sky.
At eleven,
he ambled with me through clover
from back door to clothesline,
lighting a wick in me
I hadn't known was there.

At sixteen,
he whispered what he wanted for me
in my left ear,
and I spent the rest of the day ill
in the backseat of a car.
I wondered at nineteen
if I could die for the Lord
as I stood in line, white-robed, swaying
to the choir—glory,
and he drowned me in a flood.

The Lord said "her" at a yard sale,
age twenty-six.
She handed me my change
and the story of her move.
That's when I watched a widow
weep on her kitchen floor.

At thirty-one,
I met the Lord at a lake
edged with silence and hazed peaks.
He taught me to wait.
We sat for a summer, tasted
the blazing close of lilting-blue days,
and I was full.

At thirty-six,
I tasted the Lord's absence in success—
tart, tart, tart
as a grapefruit rind.
I could not find where he lived.
Then I picked up a pen,
found him hiding
on the page calling,
calling, calling out my name
from between the lines.

> *God girds me with strength and makes my way straight.*
> —PS 18:33

Each Thought a Room in Which I Dwell

May the chambers of my mind
be a thousand fields
each with its own cloud-frescoed sky.

May the poem of each field
be a sonnet sewn in starling chatter
and quarter-rhyme.

> *May the . . . meditation of my heart be pleasing to you, O Lord.*
> —PS 19:14

May Breath Find Your Lungs

for Cozette

May morning dapple you with apricot light,

hold you like an ocean buoys a boat,

like prayer. May the womb of this world

carry you. May you loll and hum,

your five-year-old self catching tadpoles

down at the creek where the rock-green stream

muddies pant-legs, baptizes your carefully-laced

shoes. May evening blanket you. May

your sleep be sweet, watched over by stars,

whose contract is love, and the night-glow

of a small warm bulb inside an orange whelk.

> *May the Lord answer you when you are in distress.*
>
> —PS 20:1

What is This Life but a Catalogue of Sighs?

When words

dry up,

when wind

steals my breath,

when the work

for which I rise

no longer

requires my hand,

when my feet no longer hold

the ground below

this tree of bones—

let me be a note

holding out

for joy,

a cricket's trill,

a humming

in God's

throat.

> *How greatly he delights in your salvation.*
>
> —PS 21:2

Thanks for Swirled Babka

at the station café.
The pull and lurch
of the train. Traipsing
gusty blocks
to join a swaying
robed choir, glory
creased in their brows.
Prayed-over pizza
on paper plates,
mango lemonade
cloying sweet—
cheap fuel
for our Sabbath feast.
Bratwurst
and peppers
sizzling on the wind,
floating us down
the gum-gobbed stairs
at Broadway and 50th,
hallelujahs ringing in our ears,
the winter sun far gone.

> *I will praise you amid the congregation.*
>
> —PS 22:23

You Sit Me Down on a Lake–Sculpted Log

water-smooth,
wind playing marsh stalks
against the deep well of the bay
on a low-cloud day
in a town not my own.

You stay me on the shore,
the in-between, flash
of jewelwing on a bulrush,
mallards dabbling
at pickerelweed.

You bathe me in afternoon,
whitecaps scrawling the far
wild open, a buoy nodding
some lost code to joy,
a lone egret plume.

> *He leads me beside quiet waters.*
>
> —PS 23:2

The Air is the Lord's

Shetland gales
grooming treeless hills,
Mistral stunting
the lavendered Camargue,
Borneo tropic lungs, leaf-thick,
dripping rain.
The air is the Lord's:
storm columns
roaming plains, updrafts
sparked with lightning
shocking night,
zephyrs of Chernobyl
ghosting rooms of peeling paint.
The air is the Lord's:
clouds of witness
haloing Delhi, LA, Hanoi,
steam rising
from New York's city grates,
every smoke stack's
dingy bloom.

> *The earth is the Lord's and the fullness thereof.*
>
> —PS 24:1

I Wanted the Woods Like
I Wanted Something Lost

School was rattling bell, scrape
of chalk and metal desks,
glare of tile.

I wanted leaf-shade,
fir tops whispering high up,
moss greenly moist.

I wanted hidden creek—
water traveling small rocks,
in tiny tings and slurs.

I wanted the give of earth-floor
under feet, the damp breath
of sweet fern, fungi, violet cort.

One day on a shelf, a book—
sculpted cupfuls of words—
Edna St. Vincent Millay

perfectly naming exile,
whispering my forest hunger,
my woods-ward gaze.

Poem by poem,
I listened to warblers
no one else could hear,

smelled the wood rot,
touched the damp, breathed
the pine-sap air.

> *I lift up my soul.*
> —PS 25:1

Lord, I Remember

walking the woods, notes
for a sermon in hand—my first. I shaped words
into the ears of oaks, preached to every listening pine,
shivered at the prospect of speaking for God.
At the edge of the pond, a white heron
fished among tall reeds.

> *Lord, I love . . . the place where your glory dwells.*
>
> —PS 26:8

Between Car Door Closed and
Porch Light Triggered

I stilled.

Barn roof square

against night.

Snow dry-packed—*crack*

under boot,

slightest shift of weight.

Span of salt-spill sky.

The domed atlas of it all.

Ice-air pressing

lips, cheeks, face,

daring me to stay, delay,

breathe sure,

breathe deep;

pull into me

the wild dark sweep.

> *That I may dwell in the house of the Lord.*
>
> —PS 27:4

Consider

the white-lipped grove snail,
its single-footed night quest
across damp bark of downed maple.

Or the seven-petalled starflower
speckling leaf-rot,
its lance-shaped leaves
like a stilled pinwheel,
whorled delicately green.

Or the yellow-rumped warbler
feasting on wax myrtle and cold,
whistling loose in twisted scrub.

> *Consider . . . what his hands have made.*
>
> —PS 28:5

Come Like a Wrecking Ball

Come like a sundering wind.
Come like a storm-whipped
wave, dark surge
cold-claiming the shore.
Come like a night-thief
and plunder all:
the jewel of our proud
lies, the mask,
the carved-glass flask
of our dissent.
Come like fire
blazing down a high
wooded slope.
Yes, come charring
every hollow word,
torching the scaffolds
of false hope.

> *The voice of the Lord breaks the cedars.*
>
> —PS 29:5

In the Room of Illness

the walls did not listen. The clock
did not see.
The air hung empty, dead,
wrung, clean, dry.
In dreams, the ones I loved
looked down, then walked away.
I could not open my mouth.
Every hope my lips had owned
slipped silent
through the cracks of me.
My hands went blind. My bones
no longer sang.
All was static, half-light, pause.
All was stone, and closed.
The bed was hard,
the ceiling low.
In the ruins of my breath,
I woke, a broken bowl.

> *You turned away from me, and I was shattered.*
>
> —PS 30:7

Cup My Days like Water

Yours is the summer the oak
that canopied my youth
was born;
yours the moment
I glimpsed a whale
from the white-railed boat
and something in me sang;
yours the night
I floated the wide
black mouth of lake,
untethered
in salt-spilled dark;
yours the year
I feasted on loneliness—
olives, pear nectar, *pain
au chocolat;*
yours the weeks
I conferred with catbirds,
nursed a stair-fractured foot;
yours the afternoon
I saw a budding branch
in April snow—
severed—
and learned to lament;

yours the morning
I woke
from the dream
of a cottage I'd never seen
but was home.
The siding was mother-of-pearl.
Even the tulips were blue.

My times are in your hands.

—PS 31:15

In Whom There is Nothing False

Blessed is the one whose heart
is a lake the Lord makes smooth,
whose songs are night cadences,
whippoorwill's tune.

Blessed is the one whose hand
the Lord sets to work
with wood or word, whose sleep
is wax-moon full.

Blessed is the one whose foot
the land can name, who stands
humbly leaning
on what the Lord has made.

Blessed is the one whose ear
the Lord carves deep,
a cup to hold river,
wing song, breath of sheep.

> *Blessed is the one . . . in whose spirit is no deceit.*
>
> —PS 32:2

The Song Was Earth Waking

Water finding itself
no longer ice,
the neighbor's geese
asserting their claim
on snowmelt pooling
where pasture
dips and creases—
flash of wing, tail feather,
yellow beak.
The song was unmown hay,
wet, rinsed with thaw,
last summer's gold
matted down,
a crown the white world
stole, then left behind.
The song was bud
on shrub branch
waiting to be nudged
open, the blue-turning-rust
of sky bidding me
stay, the small work
of swallows
teasing the air
till evening sang.

Sing to him a new song.

—PS 33:3

Be Cactus Bloom

Be red desert blush.
Be peacock plume
glanced by high-noon sun.
Be moon-ring
chalking winter night.
Be lake silver,
mint nickel fine.
Be stove flame
oranging hot glass.
Be taffeta sheen,
jewel beetle,
burnished brass.

> *Look to him and be radiant.*
> —PS 34:5

Who is Like Maker of Beaver Tooth

fitter of wing,

the one who sings word into flesh,

footnotes night

with Venus, Jupiter, Mars,

fashions eye and to the eye appears

in parables of cumulous,

kelp forest, quartz.

Who is like issuer

of ocean, sculptor of wave?

Who is like hewer of pelican beak,

blackthorn leaf,

salamander tongue?

Who is like schemer of seed,

dreamer of fuchsia,

fashioner of gale,

the one who sets the course

for every alder root, monarch,

meteor, whale?

    Who is like you, Lord?

    —PS 35:10

The Curious Will Inherit the Earth

Pity those who never inspect
what lies beneath a given rock,

who miss out on the riddles
of feldspar, the lives of click

beetles, the parables of cricket
nymphs molting their past, leg

by leg till the body mask sloughs
off clean—perfect and perfectly

obsolete. O Lord, apprentice us
to the traceries under our feet.

> *Wisdom and goodness they deserted long ago.*
>
> —PS 36:3

Who Takes Concern for Others More Than Self?

She will preside over oaks
and podiums and choices
made under high dome.

Who hoards not, but seeks to share?

He will govern prairie and street,
hold the keys to streams, museums,
and every hidden vault.

Who refuses to lift her voice in blame?

She will helm oceans, hold court
with lions, ordain a feast
for the scammed, the trampled,
the erased.

> *The meek will inherit the land.*
>
> —PS 37:11

If I Cannot Lift My Head

let my resting be bowing.
If I cannot speak,
let my silence be prayer.
If I cannot eat, let my fast
break chains.
If my visitors
are passing clouds,
let this be communion.
If I cannot hold a book,
let the Word become light.
If I cannot wash,
let Job be my friend.
If all I hear is creak
of house beam, furnace hum,
my own throated groan,
let this be holy song.

> *I am bowed down.*
>
> —PS 38:6

What Am I

but a sequin
catching
the veiled eye
of sun—
silver-star
bright
then gone,
a six-
pointed
bit of lace-
edged ice
traveling
the white
staircase
of winter?

You have made my days a mere handbreadth.
—PS 39:5

Incarnation

He came to us in sacrament
of clothes—leather, cotton, wool:
earth reaped and twined, dyed,
cut, and sewn for the draping
      of temple—of bones.

He came to us in offering
of nail by which we glimpsed
roof holding dry, keeping warm,
boards shaved into a perfect room,
      an ark—a womb.

He came to us in liturgy of lamp
by which we knew ourselves blind
apart from light, by which the new
world broke into us like a birth:
      first fire—first life.

    Look, I have come.

    —PS 40:7

What the Lord Hears

A cello when I pray.
Water-bright tones
plucked on a harp.

The small piping
of a child's whistle—
air pressed narrowly through tin.

What conductors hear,
podium still, the moment before
lifting the baton.

What composers hear
before dotting a staff.
The notes behind the notes.

> *You know me inside and out.*
>
> —PS 41:12

Lord, I Remember

when the priest kneeled
on green carpet, dipped twelve men
and women's feet in a white, water-filled bowl,
toweled their exposed heels and toes.
Incense rose. We sang. You came
near, whispered in my ear,
friend.

> *I rehearse everything I know of you.*
>
> —PS 42:6

The Map Was a Veined Leaf

The rucksack
was my frame of bones,
into which a wealth
of questions was poured.
Everywhere
I stepped on the broad earth
was the path.

> *Give me a map, so I can find my way to the sacred mountain.*
>
> —PS 43:3

I Come to Be Broken

to leave behind
my clinging, my having
to have,
even my weeping.

Oh take me back
to the womb,
where no furniture exists
but love, no enterprise
but rest.

> *You have broken us.*
>
> —PS 44:19

He Offers You Crocus

poking through vetch
on a snow-wet day the starlings claim
with silver call.
He honors you
with round-horn sheep
who hold you in gaze, let you finger
black wool thick with oil.
He crowns your days
with poolings of rain, small ponds
jeweling the damp world.

> *God, your God, has set you above your companions*
> *by anointing you with the oil of joy.*
>
> —PS 45:7

Stand at Day's Edge

with stilled tongue.
Breathe thaw
and damp
till earth musk
crowds lungs.
Hear stone-lined
stream ting
and plink
its way to low.
Taste anise
on wind.
Wait on sky.
Know.

> *Be still, and know that I am God.*
> *—Ps 46:10*

To Dwell

To stay long
on one stretch of loam. To know
the roll and crease of field
as bend of wrist. To grow
with the land, concede to the pace
of maple, of birch.
To rest when sky says, *Rest.*
Fog bank, mica flecks, leaning fence—
to inhabit the rhetoric of place,
to love what the snow
has left.

> *He chose for us the land where we live.*
>
> —PS 47:4

To Pilgrim

To trust the road, glaring,

steep. To lean

into every dim bend

expectant

as a child

not yet bruised

by fear, not yet scraped

by voices

edged with honey and steel.

To make a friend

of loss,

glimpse yourself

fastened to the world

by a stem.

He will be our guide even to death.

—PS 48:14

Handing Over the Title

Nudge me,
and I will yield up what is mine:
a cracked locket
of spilled time, words
forged in fire
and dark, a few penny rolls
tucked away
in an airless steel vault.

Everything
I own I owe.
Loosen my knuckled grip,
and I will deed it all
to light
like a flute
offering itself to wind,
like sky
unfastening itself
of snow.

> *They will take nothing with them when they die.*
>
> —PS 49:17

A Holy Interruption is Our God

A breaking into Judean night.
Blood on straw.
A ripping open of sky.
A mule's prodigal bray and squeal.
Night terrors
in the chambers of a king.
A rap on the door.
Strangers smelling of wood smoke
and desert sheep.
A star of stars rising low—
celestial burning bush.
Riff raff drunk on praise
cantering through lonely streets,
hollering the world
from sleep.

> *May our God come and not keep silent.*
>
> —PS 50:3

What Tore in Me

was glory
made with paper and glue—
that self the self constructs
with scissors,
string, and a fifty-cent bottle
of gold.

> *Create in me a pure heart, O God.*
> —PS 51:10

Blessed are the Broke

whether by lavishness
or bad luck.
They shall be spared
the prayerlessness of the rich.
Blessed is the thin-walleted man
snoring at the back of the bus,
boot heels worn through.
Blessed is the gaunt-cheeked woman
in a faded T
sifting the one-dollar bin
at the hospital thrift.
They will be in common with Christ,
who lost his job working stone
wood, nails—
whose wealth was the Psalms,
a few good friends,
the broad earth.

> *Instead of trusting God, they trusted their wealth . . .*
> *I will trust in your good name.*
>
> —PS 52:7,9

What the Lord Sees

He searches
the high-windowed labs
of MIT, where blue-gloved
servants of cells
and polymers
scope intricate dances
through lenses.
He looks on the reeking heaps
of city waste clambered
by nimble-footed
children
who sleep under tin
in Dhaka's railroad slums.
He sees the ear-budded
sitters on planes
snoozing over the Arctic
with tonic and ice,
miles hastening beneath.
Bright-skirted women
of the Namib
winnowing wheat
with palm baskets
round as the desert sun
fall under his regard.

He notes the oyster shell courts
of Genoa and Turin,
where white-shirted men
roll polished wood balls
on level ground,
hold cigarettes to lips
between rounds.

God looks down from heaven on the entire human race.

—PS 53:2

Epitaph

In the long
second
of my life

I grew calendula
for bees
and passersby.

I wrote a prayer
someone taped
on their door.

I borrowed a bed
and my breath
and gave them back
to the Lord.

> *The Lord is the one who sustains me.*
>
> —PS 54:4

What is Prayer But a Posture?

A gesture,
a moving toward?
This morning, wordless,
I touched knees to carpet, cold,
before the work of sheets, clothes,
kindling, plants. The clock
ticked. I breathed.
That is all.

> *Every morning I will move my soul toward him.*
> —PS 55:17

Tourist as Pilgrim

In search of you, I footed cobbled hills,
folded my hands in chapels
lined with crutches and flowers, scoured
every antique alley, made a ritual of museums,
lived on baguettes, cheap brie.

In search of you, I swam a salt sea,
touched swaths of lemon holy as the sun
billowing from market booths, tasted
olives black and green, learned
to roll my *Rs*, acquired
a new name for everything.

In search of you, I slept on a train
speeding north through dark, woke on a ship
at a port white with cold, the city domed
and everyone dressed in fur,
candles the color of snow
lanterning every stone stoop.

> *You have recorded my wanderings.*
>
> —PS 56:9

I Don't Need to Climb a Mountain Before Sun-Up

to prove myself.
I don't need to cut a fine move,
catch an eye, dazzle
city glass.
I don't need a tan,
a plan for Friday night,
or jeans just right.
If I work late, it's not
because I must.
If I say *yes*, it's not
to please, steer, or feed
the hungry god
of career.
I'm through with staging.
Be gone, all masquerade!
Thank God for middle age.

> *O God, my heart is quiet and confident.*
>
> —PS 57:7

Imprecation

Let their sleep be plagued by light.
Don't bother breaking their teeth,
Lord, just their pride. May they lose
face like Saul lost his sight. No need
to melt them like wax. Just singe
the hem of their lust. Acquaint them
with dirt. Let them thirst. Prick them
with the spiny burr of truth. Turn
their trophies to dust. Uncrown
the dazzle of their youth. Feed them
the laughter of the poor. Careen them.
Let them find out what praying is for.

> *You plot injustice in your hearts.*
> *You spread violence throughout the land.*
>
> —PS 58:2

We Stepped Out of Our Lives

into silence,
which became a river.
What is prayer, after all,
but letting yourself be borne?
We shared a space
of days in which breathing slowed.
Afternoons, I dangled
my feet from the footbridge,
listened to the plink
and tumble of the brook, walked
among pines, perched
on logs, watched the lime-green
underleaves of birches lift
and quiver
till I couldn't take the beauty
any longer.

> *My strength is found when I wait upon you.*
>
> —PS 59:9

Blessed are the Confused

The habited nun
holding rosary in hand,
who hasn't heard the voice of God
in years.
The four-year-old
asking *Why?*—
holding a limp toad
in a jar.
The candled mourner
at the vigil,
no questions left.
Blessed are the holy perplexed.

Thou hast made us to drink the wine of bewilderment.

—PS 60:3

To Covenant is to Keep Turning Toward

Early, when light
slips into the waters of me
and I wake,
let me look on my love
before looking
on day.
Late, when dark
blinds me to my work
and I sleep,
let me hold my love
in the Eden
of a dream.

> *I offer you daily what I have promised.*
> —PS 61:8

I Grieve Our Lust to Fill Every Hour

To cram our waking
with making,
with heaping, with caching.
No moment wasted
dreaming, dawdling, lulling,
shooting the breeze.
I grieve the glutting of time
with looping voices
detached from tongue,
this dulling sound-circus of air.
I grieve the perpetual din
of speed, the need
to not be still,
the imperative to steal back
every stray minute
from the sin
of over-use.
I grieve the fleeing
of silence, progress
as an excuse.

> *Wait quietly before God.*
>
> —PS 62:1

At Night, You Till My Soul

Handpick small rocks,
break up clay, smooth out
the clumps, sift what is left
through quiet hands.

Hidden in the dim hour,
you work as a hushed kneader
of dough humming in the lamp-lit
backroom of a closed shop, alone.

Where your task ends, begins,
I cannot say. You travel the dark
corridors of me unseen, nameless
as a night sweeper of trains.

> *As I lie in bed, I remember you.*
>
> —PS 63:6

Confession in the Age of Scarcity Culture

I have believed the glaring industrial lie
of too little time. It has wound me up to spin
and spin. I have glittered myself with facts
designed to impress. I have inhabited the creed
I am (only) what I plot, plan, piece together
from mantras, dream scraps, free advice. Oh
save me from the lovelessness of fear. Forgive
my adultery with the gospel of more, my fierce
love affair with getting things done, my stout
allegiance to independence (the other term for
loneliness). Forgive me for scorning silence,
ignoring whisper in favor of shout. I confess
cold-shouldering rest, going AWOL from love,
high-pedestalling the antithesis of enough.

> *Surely the human heart and mind are cunning.*
>
> —PS 64:5

In the House of the Lord

was a book on a shelf with a lamp.
Open, the Lord said.
I entered the words as on a path
through a wood crosscut
with roots, winding
toward clean light.

In the house of the Lord
was a bed in a room overlooking fields.
Sleep, the Lord said.
I rested my head, leaned
against forever
like bluestem listing on wind.

In the house of the Lord
was a meal on a table of broad oak.
Eat, the Lord said.
I raised oil-dipped bread to lips.
Love has a taste.
By hunger I am saved.

> *We shall be satisfied with the goodness of your house.*
>
> —PS 65:4

Lord, I Remember

the snow-spitting day
you shattered the glass globe of my world,
then offered me a budded branch, clipped
and lying on the side of the road—
prophecy of silver-tufted wood.
I slipped it into a vase.

You have tested us, O God.

—PS 66:10

Incline My Heart to You

as high fir slope at dawn.
Draw my mind as May
draws warblers north.
Wake my eyes
to light of gentian, phlox.

I cannot tune my ear
by skill or force.
I cannot lift my gaze
but by your voice.

Call to me in stir of leaf,
drop of cone, drip of rain,
chwirk of circling hawk.

Oh say the word,
and I shall be unlocked.

> *May He make his face shine upon us.*
> —PS 67:1

To Love the World is to Mother It

To carry it on your hips,

whisper to it creed

and sky, sing over it what got stuck

in our bones before time.

To love the world is to chant

the parable

of its birth, its lover,

its lost name tossed like a coin

into the sea, waiting to be retrieved.

To love the world

is to speak its hidden name,

preach over it what foxes and warblers

know in blood, feather, and fur.

How else do we become ourselves?

> *The Lord announces the word,*
> *and the women who proclaim it are a mighty throng.*
>
> —PS 68:11

Blessed are the Worn Out

The midnight waitress
wiping down tables,
hair matted
to the back of her neck.
The white-coated lab hand
probing vile after vile
in the white-tiled room,
eyeing the institutional clock.
The black-fingered worker
of machines
whose mother lays ill.
The back-braced stocker of shelves
counting cans,
mopping up a grape juice spill.

> *I am exhausted.*
>
> —PS 69:3

Benediction

May all
who sit beside rivers
in prayer

be visited
by the white heron
of God.

    May all who search for you be filled with joy.

    —PS 70:4

Blessed are the No-Longer Young

The white-haired shuffler
doddering in the crosswalk
well after the light has changed.
The tremor-fingered sophisticate
whose baby grand rests mute
on the living room parquet.
The bifocalled puzzle whiz
in room two eighteen,
television keeping time,
a parakeet her only friend.
Blessed are all who dance
on redemption's edge.

> *In my old age, don't set me aside.*
> —PS 71:9

With a Nod to the Empty Tomb

I will make my bed.
I will seed the earth in perfect
curves and rows—
a fine labyrinth of florets
and sprouts.
I will run scales
as praise, not notes,
invoke the Triune
in every chord.
Let me slice onions,
beets, as if kitchen knives
and cutting boards
were holy art.
I will choose every word
like a glazier
perched in a high nave
carefully placing
each flame-blue shard.

> *Let the kings of Tarshish and of distant shores bring tribute to him.*
> *May the kings of Sheba and Seba present him gifts.*
>
> —PS 72:10

Lord, I Remember

scissoring felt into host
and cup, hanging my banner
on the second-row pew, listening in my plain
white dress to the priest speak in words I could not
understand. Suddenly, laughter inside: a joy
not my own—the mantle of you
covering me like snow.

> *How good it is to be near God.*
>
> —PS 73:28

Crepuscular

Give me dusk.
Fold me into lavish fade
of roof, baled hay,
pointed firs—
icons in charcoal and ash.

Let me tenant the stalling day,
dissolve into holy wait
of swallows
nested in rafters,
hawkweed curled closed.

Hold me in mauve,
in thistle-dim,
in liturgy of form and line
blurred, the far marsh's
silver wane.

I wish to mind
the simple shapes of things
again, know myself
as mere,
as shiver, as trace.

> *The day is yours, and yours also the night.*
> —PS 74:16

I See the Name of God

in the vein-code
of a leaf, hear it in the bleating
of the neighbor's round-horn sheep—
noses to grass,
going about their holy work.
I touch the name of God on bark,
feel his name firm
beneath my feet, taste it on snow,
on rain—also blackberries,
wild, plucked by a child
from bramble knotted with blossoms
white and thorned.
I hear it echo in porch chimes,
the ballads of catbirds,
the coming of storms.

> *We praise you God, for your name is near.*
> —PS 75:1

Bible Translations

Ps 1:2	Message		Ps 28:5	GW
Ps 2:8	NLT		Ps 29:5	NLV
Ps 3:3	NLT		Ps 30:7	NLT
Ps 4:3	NIV		Ps 31:15	NLV
Ps 5:3	Message		Ps 32:2	NIV
Ps 6:2	NKJV		Ps 33:3	NLV
Ps 7:6	Voice		Ps 34:5	ISV
Ps 8:4	NIrV		Ps 35:10	NIV
Ps 9:1	GNT		Ps 36:3	Voice
Ps 10:1	NLT		Ps 37:11	NIV
Ps 11:4	NIV		Ps 38:6	NIV
Ps 12:3	NIV		Ps 39:5	NIV
Ps 13:1	NLV		Ps 40:4	NIV
Ps 14:2	CSB		Ps 41:12	Message
Ps 15:2	NLT		Ps 42:6	Message
Ps 16:11	WEB		Ps 43:3	Message
Ps 17:15	NIV		Ps 44:19	ESV
Ps 18:33	TLV		Ps 45:7	NIV
Ps 19:14	NLT		Ps 46:10	NIV
Ps 20:1	NIV		Ps 47:4	GNT
Ps 21:2	TLV		Ps 48:14	WEB
Ps 22:23	TLV		Ps 49:17	NIV
Ps 23:2	NIV		Ps 50:3	NASB
Ps 24:1	ESV		Ps 51:10	NIV
Ps 25:1	NLV		Ps 52:9	CEV
Ps 26:8	NIV		Ps 53:2	NLT
Ps 27:4	NIV		Ps 54:3	NIV

Ps 55:17   PT

Ps 56:9   TLV

Ps 57:7   LB

Ps 58:2   NLT

Ps 59:9   PT

Ps 60:3   DT

Ps 61:8   GNT

Ps 62:1   NLT

Ps 63:6   GNT

Ps 64:5   NIV

Ps 65:4   NASB

Ps 66:10   NLT

Ps 67:1   NLV

Ps 68:11   NIV

Ps 69:3   NLT

Ps 70:4   NLT

Ps 71:9   LB

Ps 72:10   NIV

Ps 73:28   NLT

Ps 74:16   NIV

Ps 75:1   NIV

Acknowledgments

Thanks to the editors of the following publications, where these poems, some in an earlier form, first appeared:

> *Amethyst Review*—"To Love the World Is to Mother It,"
> "With a Nod to the Empty Tomb"

> *Anglican Theological Review*—"Opening" ("I Remember"),
> "Curtain Me in Silence"

> *Ekstasis*—"Praise for Warm Babka" ("Thanks for Swirled Babka")

> *The Reformed Journal*—"Be Cactus Bloom," "I See the Name of God"

> *Soul-Lit*—"If I Cannot Lift My Head"

> *Windhover*—"Darkness Snagged My Bones," "What the Lord Hears"

Penning poetry, for me, has always been a matter of entering into conversation with the poetry of others. In addition to holding conversation with the biblical Psalms, the poems in this collection hold conversation with the poems of Nicholas Samaras in *American Psalm, World Psalm,* which I read frequently while preparing this manuscript. Thanks to D. S. Martin for introducing me to Samaras's fine work and for believing in this project, spawned by the recommendation. Additionally, I would like to express deep gratitude to the friends and fellow writers who have helped shape the journey of these poems through thoughtful workshopping and careful editing: Gayle Heaslip, Maria Roemhildt, Meg Smith, Jeremy Stefano, and Michelle Wiegers, with special thanks to Leslie Williams and Paul J. Pastor.

The Poiema Poetry Series

Six Sundays Toward a Seventh by Sydney Lea
Epitaphs for the Journey by Paul Mariani
Within This Tree of Bones by Robert Siegel
Particular Scandals by Julie L. Moore
Gold by Barbara Crooker
A Word In My Mouth by Robert Cording
Say This Prayer into the Past by Paul Willis
Scape by Luci Shaw
Conspiracy of Light by D.S. Martin
Second Sky by Tania Runyan
Remembering Jesus by John Leax
What Cannot Be Fixed by Jill Pelaez Baumgaertner
Still Working It Out by Brad Davis
The Hatching of the Heart by Margo Swiss
Collage of Seoul by Jae Newman
Twisted Shapes of Light by William Jolliff
These Intricacies by David Harrity
Where the Sky Opens by Laurie Klein
True, False, None of the Above by Marjorie Maddox
The Turning Aside anthology edited by D.S. Martin
Falter by Marjorie Stelmach
Phases by Mischa Willett
Second Bloom by Anya Krugovoy Silver
Adam, Eve, & the Riders of the Apocalypse anthology edited by D.S. Martin
Your Twenty-First Century Prayer Life by Nathaniel Lee Hansen
Habitation of Wonder by Abigail Carroll
Ampersand by D.S. Martin
Full Worm Moon by Julie L. Moore
Ash & Embers by James A. Zoller
The Book of Kells by Barbara Crooker